The Discovery of
TUTANKHAMUN'S TOMB

The Discovery of
TUTANKHAMUN'S TOMB

Text by Howard Carter
Photographs by Harry Burton
Edited by Polly Cone

The Metropolitan Museum of Art

DISTRIBUTED BY GROSSET & DUNLAP
A Filmways Company
Publishers • New York

Library of Congress catalog card number: 77-84859
ISBN 0-448-14546-4 (paperback edition)
ISBN 0-448-14554-5 (hardcover edition)
First printing 1977
Printed in the United States of America

1978 PRINTING

The Discovery of Tutankhamun's Tomb, originally published as *Wonderful Things: The Discovery of Tutankhamun's Tomb,* is abridged and adapted from *The Tomb of Tut Ankh Amen,* by Howard Carter and A. C. Mace, 3 vols., 1923-1933. Vol. 2 used by permission of Cooper Square Publishers, Inc., New York. Photographs on cover, frontispiece, pp. 5, 21, 26, 27, 29, 42, 45, 56, 62 by courtesy of the Griffith Institute, Ashmolean Museum, Oxford; on p. 3 by courtesy of the Carnarvon family; on pp. v, xxv, 38, 84 by courtesy of *The Illustrated London News and Sketch Ltd.;* on pp. xii, xvii, xxiii, 1, 4, 6, 7, 9, 10 from the guestbook, The Metropolitan Museum of Art Expedition house, Thebes. Captions on pp. 31, 50 by courtesy of *The Illustrated London News and Sketch, Ltd.* Excerpts from *The New York Times* used by permission of the Times Newspapers Limited; The Times (London) World Copyright, by Arrangement with the Earl of Carnarvon; Special cable to *The New York Times.*

Published on the occasion of the exhibition *Treasures of Tutankhamun* at the National Gallery of Art, Washington, D.C.; Field Museum of Natural History and the Oriental Institute of the University of Chicago; New Orleans Museum of Art; Los Angeles County Museum of Art; Seattle Art Museum; and The Metropolitan Museum of Art, New York: 1976-1979.

The exhibition is made possible by a grant from the National Endowment for the Humanities and matching grants from Exxon Corporation and the Robert Wood Johnson, Jr. Charitable Trust.

Editor: Polly Cone

Designers: Arlene Goldberg and Polly Cone
Printer of the original edition: The Leether Press, Boston
Cartographer: Joseph P. Ascherl

Special photographer: Nathan Rabin

Prologue

We once had the pleasure of entertaining Rudyard Kipling at the headquarters of our Expedition in Thebes. He described the life of the field archaeologist very happily by saying: "It furnishes a scholarly pursuit with all the excitement of a gold prospector's life." That goes far toward explaining why a sporting gentleman like the late Earl of Carnarvon was willing to spend so much money and so many discouraging years looking for an unplundered tomb in the Valley of the Tombs of the Kings.

AMBROSE LANSING Assistant Curator, Egyptian Department,
The Metropolitan Museum of Art, 1923

Lord Carnarvon (second from left) with his daughter, Lady Evelyn Herbert, Howard Carter, and A. R. Callender at the mouth of the tomb

Contents

Editor's Note

This is the first pictorial account of the 1922 discovery of Tutankhamun's tomb since the illustrated newspapers of the day carried the story as it happened. Fortunately for those who missed the original coverage, Harry Burton's 1400 glass negatives made in and around the tomb over the course of six years have been preserved at The Metropolitan Museum of Art. A selection of prints from them is presented here in the order they were made.

For the text I have borrowed from *The Tomb of Tut-Ankh-Amen* by Howard Carter and A. C. Mace, first published in 1923. Who better than Carter, who discovered the tomb, could describe the pictures that were made as his excavation progressed? The captions not otherwise credited are in his words. I have culled the other caption material from letters to and from those involved in the find and from the mass of contemporary press clippings.

My gratitude goes to Charles K. Wilkinson, Curator Emeritus of Near Eastern Art at the Metropolitan Museum and a member of the Museum's Egyptian Expedition at the time of the discovery. A patient man and kind friend, he graciously served as my personal historian for the events described in these pages. The foreword he wrote conveys a fine sense of archaeology in Egypt in the 1920s and elucidates the vital part the Museum played in the matter of Tutankhamun's tomb before and after 1922. It was also Mr. Wilkinson who showed me the illustrated guestbook of the Museum Egyptian Expedition house in Thebes. I have reproduced snapshots from the book to complement Burton's excavation photographs; together I hope they may provide a visual "rediscovery" of the tomb of Tutankhamun.

P. C.

Foreword

By CHARLES K. WILKINSON
*Curator Emeritus of Near
Eastern Art, The Metropolitan
Museum of Art, and member of
the Egyptian Expedition, 1920-1931*

In the fall of 1922 the systematic persistence of Howard Carter (under the aegis of Lord Carnarvon) in seeking the tomb of Tutankhamun was rewarded, and so amply rewarded, that help—urgent help—was a necessity. An archaeological find of any importance demands instant and continuous action and the employment of various skills if preservation rather than destruction is to prevail. Nothing was more natural than that the help Carter and Carnarvon received after their discovery should have come in very great part from the Egyptian Expedition of The Metropolitan Museum of Art under the founding curatorship of Albert M. Lythgoe.

In 1911 Lythgoe had acquired for the Museum a concession that included the valley (known as the Asasif) leading to the temples at Deir el Bahri (see map, inside back cover). This concession adjoined that of the Valley of the Kings, which in 1914 was granted to Lord Carnarvon. Both concessions were on the west bank of the Nile opposite the town now called Luxor. As will be seen shortly, the men operating these two concessions were far more than simply neighbors.

Herbert Winlock, an early member of the Egyptian Expedition, had begun to work at the Metropolitan concession before World War I, and it was under his supervision that a house was erected in 1912. J. P. Morgan underwrote the expense and ordered the house built in such a manner that the members of the Museum staff dwelled simply but well; Morgan was of the opinion that the quality of work was never improved by uncomfortable living. (The opposite sentiment was the *modus vivendi* of Sir Flinders Petrie, the grand old man of English archaeology, who inflicted spartan housing on all who worked for him.)

The Museum house was practical, had a certain distinction, and bore some affinity with Coptic architecture due to the early work of Winlock at Kharga Oasis and Palmer Jones, the architect, in the Wadi Natrun—both sites yielding Coptic material. The living room was surmounted by a dome on pendentives, and the space between two of the piers was closed by a pierced wooden screen as in a Coptic church, behind which instead of a *haikal* (sanctuary) was a dining room. The house was known as the "American House," and many visitors, as the guestbook they signed attests, were entertained there. Thanks to the encouragement of J. P. Morgan—and the taste of those who materialized his wishes—none who entered its portals could feel that they had been slumming or boast that they had roughed it. When, by order of the Museum trustees, the concession was relinquished in 1947, it was the sad duty of Walter Hauser and myself—both of us members of the Egyptian Expedition in the 1920s—to hand the house over to the Egyptian department of antiquities. Scholars board in it to this day.

Howard Carter was no stranger in this house, and here many conversations took place even before his great find. Carter's interests and those of the Metropolitan Museum had become interwoven, as Carter had once worked in what became the Museum's concession. He had even discovered a gigantic royal tomb there in 1900; it produced an empty coffin and a somewhat repulsive statue of King Mentjuhotpe (2060-2010 B.C.). Carter had not only copied some of the colored reliefs of the Eighteenth Dynasty temple of Queen Hatshepsut (1503-1483 B.C.), which Winlock had excavated at Deir el Bahri, but had an intimate knowledge of the whole area of the Valley of the Kings.

Furthermore, Winlock and Carter were both fully aware that positive evidence had been found in the Valley to prove that a tomb of Tutankhamun existed there. It was Winlock who had examined the cache of pottery and linens Theodore M. Davis had found in 1908 in a pit near the site of Tutankhamun's tomb. Winlock positively identified the find as materials left over from the embalming of the young king. Naturally, then, after several unproductive years of excavation for Lord Carnarvon, Carter sought help at the American House in reassuring Carnarvon that the search was not in vain.

Domed living room of the Metropolitan Museum Egyptian Expedition house in Thebes

THE EASTERN TELEGRAPH COMPANY, LIMITED.

(Message Forms 5/17.)

Clerk's Name.

LONDON STATIONS:—

ELECTRA HOUSE,
FINSBURY PAVEMENT, E.C. 2 ...
115, CANNON STREET, E.C. 4 ...
8, LEADENHALL STREET, E.C. 3...
THE BALTIC,
BURY ST. ENTRANCE, E.C. 3 ...

(3240
London Wall)

29, MINCING LANE, E.C. 3 } MARKET }
26, MARK LANE, E.C. 3 } BLDGS. }
37, HOLBORN VIADUCT, E.C. 1 ...
41 & 42, PARLIAMENT STREET, S.W. 1... (2516 Gerrard)
6, DENMAN STREET, BOROUGH, S.E. 1 (2942 Hop.)

(3240
London Wall)

ISSUED FROM

41/42, PARLIAMENT STREET, S.W. 1.

No. _14_

REMARKS.

_Rp 12_

No. _____ 19

The following TELEGRAM Received at _____ J. J8

From _Cairo_ _____ via " Eastern."

Foreign No. } No. of Words } _38_ Dated _7_ Time _____ m.

To _Rp12 Lythgoe Brown Shipley_

Pall Mall Ln

Thanks message discovery
colossal and need every
assistance could you
consider loan of burton
in recording in time being
costs to us immediate reply
would oblige every regards carter Continental
Cairo

REPLIES SHOULD BE ORDERED *Via Eastern*

Doubtful words should be officially repeated. See Rule Book.

☞ No inquiry respecting this Telegram can be attended to without the production of this Copy.

Waterlow & Sons Limited, London Wall, London. (665-451.)

Lythgoe, in his self-abnegating style, was a master at getting his own way. It was a result of his efforts that the loan of the Museum staff to Carter was fully endorsed by the trustees and Edward Robinson, the director. As head of the Egyptian Department, Lythgoe was well aware of the close links between Carter's operations and the Museum's own; a firm believer in the value of his profession and the

Form for Deferred Plain Language Telegrams.

E. T. Co. : LONDON.

TELEPHONE NUMBER: } 3632 LONDON WALL.

TELEGRAPHIC ADDRESS: } "SIGNALLY, AVE, LONDON."

THE EASTERN TELEGRAPH COMPANY LIMITED

No. .	Words.
Date. Dec. 7. 1922.	Sent at ___ No. and Circuit ___
Code Time.	Charge. £ s. d.	By

Via Eastern Official Instructions

NOTICE :—This Telegram cannot be accepted unless the Declaration at the foot of the Telegram is previously filled in and signed by the Sender.

To Receiver's Name *L C* Carter, Hotel Continental, Cairo

Address _____

Only too delighted to assist in every possible way. Please call upon Burton and any other members of our staff. Am cabling Burton to that effect.

Lythgoe.

I hereby declare that the text of the above Telegram is entirely in plain language (the language used being*_____ and that it does not bear any meaning other than that which appears on the face of it.

I request that the Telegram may be forwarded on the faith of the foregoing declaration and subject to the conditions printed on the back hereof by which I agree to be bound.

Signature and Address of Sender *A.M. Lythgoe, Burlington Hotel*

(Not to be telegraphed.) * State here the language used

Left margin: To prevent mistakes attention is called to the importance of legible writing.

Left margin: All important Telegrams should be repeated.—Quarter-rates extra charged for Repetition.

importance of professional cooperation, he was quick to offer the fullest help when Carter requested it immediately after the discovery. The four Expedition staff members whom Carter borrowed all operated out of the American House. With that, of course, even closer ties with Carter were established.

Lythgoe was a great believer in photography in archaeology and relied on it probably more than any other excavator. He was thus well aware why Carter was so anxious to have Harry Burton's help. Carter had known Burton, who, like himself, was from Norfolk, England, not in that country but in Egypt, since before 1914. Burton had photographed for—and had even done some excavating in the Valley of the Kings for—Theodore M. Davis, one of the first American patrons of archaeology in Egypt and a great benefactor of the Metropolitan Museum. Burton's talents were most attractive for Howard Carter's purposes: not only was he highly skilled professionally but was known for his calm temper—even under strain.

By arranging for Ambrose Lansing to take charge of the Metropolitan's dig at El Lisht to the north, Lythgoe freed Arthur Mace to help Carter also. Both Mace and Carter had been associated with Sir Flinders Petrie; Mace, another Englishman, was a cousin of Petrie, and Carter was one of the many Egyptologists who had their initial training under Petrie. Carter and Mace were both meticulous in every way; their education and knowledge being somewhat different, they formed an ideal working partnership which was broken only by Mace's failing health.

Lindsley Hall and Walter Hauser, both from the Massachusetts Institute of Technology and fully experienced on the Metropolitan's Expeditions, were released by Winlock for their less extensive but most necessary help as draftsmen. In a jumble of objects, photographs without supplementary isometric drawings are not enough.

Despite the enormous concentration of archaeological and other attention on Tutankhamun from 1922 for several years, other Egyptological work went on more or less as usual—including that of the Metropolitan's own two Expeditions. Winlock continued to superintend the excavations in the valley of the Asasif, producing several small statues of Queen Hatshepsut, and went to Cairo when it was necessary to help Carter negotiate with the Egyptian authorities. In 1925 the expedition from the Museum of Fine Arts, Boston, and Harvard University, working among the pyramids of Giza, found a royal tomb of Queen Hetepheres (about 2600 B.C.), and though she was missing, her funerary furniture was not. But, unquestionably, Tutankhamun held the spotlight. Both good and bad aspects of this attention were observable in the American House, and life there was no longer one with but occasional visitors. Accompanying the increase in visitors to Luxor was a great deal of publicity.

Typical tourist conveyance
in Thebes

The tradition among Egyptologists was that their work be conducted in privacy as it required the full attention of those engaged in it and that publication of their work and their finds was their privilege and, eventually, their duty. It requires no imagination to realize the deluge of intrusions Carter faced, even though he eventually had the aid of a friend who acted as private secretary, and whose job—to quote the quip of the time—was to tell people to go to hell politely. Even so, in the first three months of 1926, after much of the contents of the tomb had gone to the Cairo Museum, no fewer than 20,000 people visited the tomb, and over 270 passed through the laboratory where delicate work was still being done.

Luxor during those years was full of tourists and journalists, although there were no airplanes, and, after an initial journey by rail or boat, most visits to the tomb were made on donkeyback or in carriages. Of these visitors some were gratified and many frustrated. All were vocal, and fact and rumor were not always distinguishable. One of the rumors concerned the American House, which was said to contain in its storerooms Tutankhamun's queen! As a result, thieves tunneled into one of the storerooms during the off-season and found empty cartons and broken pottery for their pains. The press was so effective that Winlock, then in New York, read of the break-in in the New York papers forty-eight hours after it had occurred.

There were some pleasant aspects of all the attention. Carter's find drew to the scene—and for the most part to the American House—the preeminent Egyptologists of the day, including James H. Breasted, Alan Gardiner, and Percy Newberry—all famous in their particular fields. In addition came scientists with related interests and people distinguished in other ways. The discussions and conversations beneath that domed roof and in the "sanctuary" of the dining room were widened and enriched as never before.

One visitor particularly affected was Edward S. Harkness, a longtime friend and supporter of Lythgoe. Harkness was also a trustee and later president of the board at the Metropolitan Museum. His interest in Egyptian art was so increased by his stay in Egypt that in 1926, after Lord Carnarvon's death, he presented Carnarvon's exquisite collection to the Museum. Through Harkness's generosity Carnarvon's personal treasures of Egyptian art, which he began to assemble in 1907 and completed before the discovery of Tutankhamun's tomb, may now be enjoyed by all who trouble to see them.

The early 1920s was a time of great change; after the conclusion of the First World War, national consciousness was on the rise in many parts of the world, including Egypt. This in its turn affected archaeology, and it is interesting that the age of privately financed excavation ended with Carnarvon's concession in the Valley of the Kings. Through the understanding and beneficence of Lord Carnarvon and the expertise of Carter, the era of excavation in Egypt under personal patronage—which had not always satisfied scientific standards—was brought to a glorious conclusion. Albert Lythgoe, in giving Carnarvon and Carter so much assistance from the Metropolitan Museum Egyptian Expedition, helped make the transition to a more academic and institutionalized era easier than it could otherwise have been. Now carefully treated and preserved, Tutankhamun's body, his gold coffin, and objects ranging from the most opulent treasures to a simple reed he cut with his own hand are the proud possessions of Egypt, his own land.

Albert M. Lythgoe and Edward S. Harkness in Egypt

Introduction

This article was written by ARTHUR C. MACE for the Metropolitan Museum's Bulletin of December 1923, at the beginning of the second season of work at Tutankhamun's tomb

Lord Carnarvon's and Howard Carter's discovery of the tomb of Tutankhamun has aroused an interest, not merely in this particular find, but in archaeology generally, that to the excavator is almost embarrassing. Ordinarily he spends his time quietly and unobtrusively enough, half the year burrowing mole-like in the ground, and the other half writing dull papers for scientific journals, and now suddenly he finds himself in the full glare of the limelight, with newspaper reporters lying in wait for him at every corner, and snapshotters recording his every movement. He can not even hammer in a nail without five continents knowing all about it by breakfast time next morning. It is, as I said, embarrassing and a little bewildering, and the excavator feels sometimes that he would like to know why the ordinary details of his daily work should suddenly have become of intense and absorbing interest to the world at large. Why is it? Whence has the ordinary every-day citizen derived this sudden enthusiasm for the funeral furniture of a long-dead Pharaoh?

The explanation is, I suppose, simple enough really. It lies in the fact that we are all, even the most prosaic of us, children under our skins, and thrill deliciously at the very idea of buried treasure. Sealed doorways, jeweled robes, inlay of precious stones, kings' regalia—the phrases grip, and we can now, under cover of scientific interest, openly and unashamedly indulge an intellectual appetite that has hitherto been nourished surreptitiously on detective stories and murder cases in the press. Now at last we can claim open fellowship with John Silver's parrot, and gabble our "pieces of eight, pieces of eight" without shame. How Stevenson, by the way, would have loved excavating.

In view of this widespread interest and the general familiarity with Tutankhamun's name, it comes as almost a shock to find how little we really know about this monarch. Before the finding of the tomb he was little more than a name, and even now, though we know with almost embarrassing detail the extent of his possessions, we are still almost entirely in the dark as to his origin, his life, and his personal character.

He became king (about 1334 B.C.) by virtue of his marriage with Ankhesenpaaton, third daughter of the so-called heretic king, Akhenaton, but we have at present no means of telling whether the marriage took place during Akhenaton's lifetime, or was contracted hastily after his death to give Tutankhamun a pretext for seizing the throne. It was not, one would have thought, a particularly enviable or safe position to aspire to at this juncture, for the country was in a state of chaos, and the people were seething with discontent. In his short reign Akhenaton "The Dreamer" had thrown away an empire, and alienated nine-tenths of his own subjects, and now at his death there was no obvious person to succeed him. Sons he had none, and our interest centers upon a group of girls, his daughters. The eldest of these, Meritaton, had been married a year or two before her father's death to a certain Smenkhara, a vague person of whom we know nothing but the facts that he acted as co-regent with Akhenaton during the last year or two of his reign, and that he disappears from the scene immediately after Akhenaton's death. This latter circumstance is suspicious, to say the least of it. In oriental countries coincidences of this nature are generally very carefully arranged beforehand, and it is more than likely that Smenkhara was quietly and effectively—what shall we say?—abolished.

The second daughter died in Akhenaton's lifetime, and the third was the Ankhesenpaaton who was married to our king.

It must have been immediately obvious to Tutankhamun or to his advisers that a complete surrender must be made of all Akhenaton's ideas and principles, an unconditional return to the old order and the old gods, if the country was to recover from the chaos into which it had lapsed. In pursuance of this policy Tell el Amarna, the heretic capital, was abandoned, the Court was transferred back again to Thebes, the new king changed his name from Tutankhaton to Tutankhamun, and the favor of the powerful priests was courted by putting in hand restorations and additions to the Amun temples. How far these concessions to popular opinion were effectual we do not know, but that they must have gone some way towards stabilizing the government of the country is evident from the scenes in the tomb of one of the king's viceroys, Huy by name, wherein both Syrians and Nubians are represented as bringing tribute to Tutankhamun's Court.

That exhausts the facts of Tutankhamun's life as we know them from the monuments. The rest is pure conjecture. We do not even know the length of his reign—in fact, the one dated object we possess, a piece of inscribed cloth of the sixth year, is in our own Metropolitan Museum collection. We have reason to believe that he was little more than a boy when he died, and that it was his successor, Ay, who supported his candidature to the throne and acted as his adviser during his brief reign. It was Ay, moreover, who arranged his funeral ceremonies.

The tomb was situated in the center of the Valley of the Kings, not very far from the spot in which Theodore M. Davis had found the famous cache, a group of royal funerary objects from Tell el Amarna, brought to Thebes on the abandonment of the heretic capital, and hidden away in this spot, as the clay sealings would seem to indicate, by Tutankhamun himself. Nor was other evidence lacking to connect Tutankhamun with this particular part of the Valley. Nearby Mr. Davis had found, hidden under a stone, a faience cup with the name of our king upon it, and in a small pit-tomb some fragments of gold foil which bore the names both of Tutankhamun and of his queen. Another of his finds was even more significant and, as it happens, nearly concerns our own Museum. This was a cache of large pottery sealed jars, buried in an irregular hole a little way eastwards from the Akhenaton cache. There was nothing to show to which tomb, if any, the jars belonged, and, as they seemed to contain nothing but bundles of linen, broken fragments of pottery, and other miscellaneous rubbish, they were passed over and stored away. A year or two later H. E. Winlock noticed these jars in one of Mr. Davis's storerooms, and realized from a hasty examination of the contents that there might be interesting information to be gleaned from them. Through the kind offices of Harry Burton, who was then working with Mr. Davis, they were handed over to him with the permission of the Egyptian authorities and shipped home to New York, and in the Museum he made a thorough investigation of their contents. They proved to be even more interesting than he had anticipated. There were the remains of a great number of plain and decorated pottery vases; there were headshawls and other pieces of linen, one of which was inscribed with the date of the sixth year of Tutankhamun as mentioned above; and, most significant of all, there were a number of clay sealings, some bearing the name of Tutankhamun, and others the impression of the Royal Necropolis Seal, the jackal and nine captives. It was a curious jumble of material, but there seemed good reason for supposing that it came from a tomb of Tutankhamun somewhere in the neighborhood, and represented the final gathering up of oddments after the funeral ceremonies, or, more probably, considering the rough treatment it had undergone, a hasty collection of scattered fragments after the tomb had been plundered. Had we known then, as we know now, that the two seal-impressions found within the jars were identical with those with which the tomb had been originally closed and subsequently re-sealed, we should have had no doubt about the matter.

Lord Carnarvon and Mr. Carter had, then, considerable grounds for believing that the tomb of Tutankhamun was situated in this particular part of the Valley, and for many reasons his was the tomb they most hoped to find. They searched for it for several seasons and removed several thousand tons of debris without success, and not the least dramatic part of the whole discovery is the fact that it was made in a last effort, when hope was almost dead. At the end of the season of 1921-22 it became a matter of serious debate for them whether, after so many barren years of work, it would not be better to abandon the Valley and try their luck elsewhere, and they finally decided to return for one more season, a short season of two months only. Then, on November 4, just five days after the work had been started, the tomb was found.

Photography was the first and most pressing need at the outset, for it was absolutely essential that a complete photographic record of the objects in the tomb should be made before anything was touched. This part of the work was undertaken by Burton, and the wonderful results he achieved are known to every one, his photographs having appeared in most of the illustrated papers throughout the world. They were all taken by electric light, wires having been laid to connect the tomb with the main lighting system of the Valley, and for a darkroom, appropriately enough, he had the unfinished tomb which Tutankhamun had used as cache for the funerary remains of the Tell el Amarna royalties.

Harry Burton photographing in Thebes

Lindsley Hall and Walter Hauser were responsible for the plan of the tomb. Each individual object was drawn to scale in the exact position in which it lay, and a reference to the photographs of the interior, which illustrate the confused and haphazard manner in which these objects were piled one upon another, will give some idea of the difficulties that confronted them.

Mace (foreground, left) at work in his tomb laboratory

My own share of the work was largely confined to the laboratory, which was established, with the consent of the Department of Antiquities, in the tomb of Sety II, conveniently situated in a secluded spot at the extreme end of the Valley. Here, working in collaboration with Mr. Lucas, Director of the Government Chemical Laboratories, who most generously sacrificed three months' leave to come and help us, and whose chemical knowledge was invaluable, I spent the greater part of the winter, receiving the objects as one by one they were brought up out of the tomb, noting and cataloguing them, and carrying out such repairs and restorations as were necessary.

Carter (left) securing a couch for transport to the laboratory

The most exciting of the laboratory tasks was the unpacking of the boxes and caskets, for, owing to the confused nature of their contents, you could never be certain of anything, and at any moment, tucked away in a corner, or concealed in the fold of a garment, you might come across a magnificent scarab or piece of jewelry, or a wonderful statuette. The jumble was amazing, the most incongruous things being packed together, and for some time we were completely in the dark as to its meaning. The explanation, as we worked it out later, is as follows:

Some years after the burial of the king, plunderers had contrived to tunnel their way into the tomb and had made a hurried and ruthless search for treasure that was portable, ransacking the boxes and throwing their contents all over the floor. Then, probably while the plunderers were still at work, the officials responsible for the safe-keeping of the royal necropolis got wind of the affair, and came post-haste to investigate. Some of the thieves made good their escape—the faience cup beneath the rock which we referred to above was probably hidden by one of them—but others were evidently either caught on the spot, or apprehended later with the loot still in their possession. Then came the question of making good the damage, and a hurried and perfunctory job the officials seem to have made of it. No attempt was made to re-sort the material or pack the objects back into the boxes that were originally intended for them. Instead, they were gathered up in handfuls and bundles and hastily crammed into the nearest box. As a result we get the most incongruous mixtures, walking-sticks and underlinen, jewelry and faience vases, headrests and robes of state.

From the point of view of our laboratory work it would have been far better if the contents of the boxes had been left lying as the thieves had scattered them. As repacked they were extraordinarily difficult to handle, and one had to exercise constant care lest, in removing an object from an upper layer, one did some damage to a still more valuable object which lay beneath. Nor was it always possible to remove one single piece at a time, for in the sweeping-up process a number of the objects inevitably became tangled and interfolded, with the result that in some cases three or four garments were so hopelessly involved that they had to be treated as one. What this meant in dealing with heavily decorated robes, of which the actual cloth was in such bad condition that it could not even be touched, and when the only chance of working out the size and shape was by noting the exact scheme of decoration, will more readily be comprehended when I explain that it took three weeks of hard work to clear a single box.

Slow and exacting the work was, but intensely interesting, and worth every minute of the time that was spent upon it. No trouble could be too great, for we have been given an opportunity such as archaeology has never known before, and in all probability will never see again. Now for the first time we have what every excavator has dreamt of, but never hoped to see, a royal tomb with all its furniture intact. The increase to our sum of archaeological knowledge should be enormous, and we, as a Museum, should count it as a privilege to have been able to take such a prominent part in the work.

Some idea of the extent of the discovery may be gleaned from the fact that the objects so far removed represent but a quarter of the contents of the tomb, and that, probably, the least valuable quarter. We have cleared the antechamber. There remain the burial chamber, the treasury, and the annex, and, to all appearance, each contains far finer objects than any we have handled yet. It is the first of these chambers that will occupy us in the opening months of the coming season. There, beneath the sepulchral shrines, three thousand years ago the king was laid to rest, and there, or ever these words appear in print, we hope to find him lying.

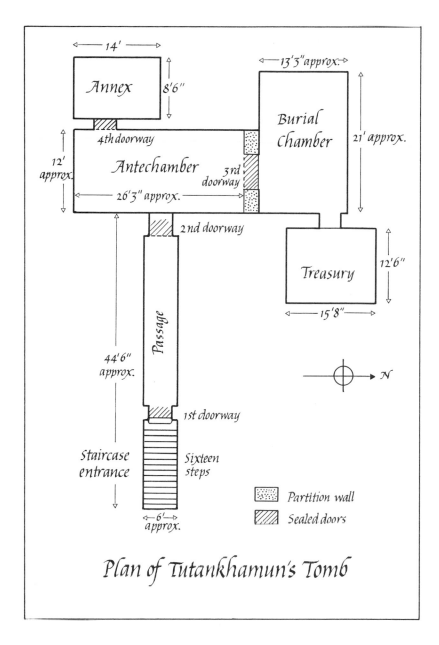

Plan of Tutankhamun's Tomb

You will have gained an idea from the numerous descriptions in the newspapers as to the arrangement of the chambers so far as they are yet known. The entrance passage (some 40 feet long) leads into a 1st antechamber in the middle of its eastern side. The chamber measures about 26 x 12 feet. In the opposite (western) side of this 1st antechamber, a doorway, somewhat to the left of the middle of that wall, opens into a 2nd antechamber. Then to one's right as he still stands in the entrance doorway to the tomb, the north wall of that 1st antechamber is pierced by another doorway (still sealed and unopened) leading into what is unquestionably the tomb proper—i.e. the sepulchral chamber or chambers.

Letter, Lythgoe to Robinson, 1 February 1923

The Men

Our men are doing a magnificent piece of work, and this whole procedure is running with clocklike regularity. Burton is the only one, who, with all his past experience behind him, could have possibly made such a marvellously fine record for all time by photography. Mace's careful and painstaking methods are producing an unparalleled series of notes and records, minute in every detail, while Hauser's and Hall's drawings and plans, giving the positions of the objects, round out the completeness of the record to the Nth degree! It is fortunate indeed for posterity that our organization could have slipped into the breach on such an occasion, for it is universally acknowledged that the Museum's Expedition alone was equipped and competent to cope with the situation.

Letter, Lythgoe to Robinson, 1 February 1923

Harry Burton and Howard Carter in Luxor

HOWARD CARTER, 1873-1939

The son of an English animal painter and himself an accomplished watercolorist, Carter combined the sensibilities of artist and archaeologist to brilliant advantage. His years in Egypt began in the fall of 1891 as a draftsman at the excavations of the Egypt Exploration Fund at Beni Hasan and El Bersha with Percy Newberry. At the end of the season he had his first exposure to actual digging—at Tell el Amarna under Sir Flinders Petrie. With that he determined to become an archaeologist, and he did so by acquiring experience with the best teams then excavating in Egypt. By 1899 Carter had joined Sir Gaston Maspero in the Egyptian government department of antiquities as chief inspector of the Theban necropolis. In that capacity he worked in the Valley of the Kings with Theodore M. Davis in 1902. Later, in 1907, Davis hired Carter to draw the most important objects he had excavated at Biban el Muluk.

Sir Gaston Maspero introduced Carter to Carnarvon in 1907, and the two worked together for fifteen years, suspending active digging only during wartime. The partnership produced the crowning achievement of both men's careers with the discovery of Tutankhamun's tomb in 1922.

GEORGE EDWARD STANHOPE MOLYNEUX HERBERT, FIFTH EARL OF CARNARVON 1866-1923

Lord Carnarvon was the only son of a statesman and classics scholar, but scholarship was not his own forte. Following an undistinguished career at Eton and Cambridge, young Carnarvon, a modest man of droll good humor and impeccable taste, embarked as a world traveler, bibliophile, art collector, and fancier of racing—by horse and car. A nearly fatal automobile accident at the turn of the century determined the direction of Carnarvon's later life; the wreck permanently weakened his always frail health and forced him to flee the damp British winters. He withdrew to Egypt where archaeology became a passion. In 1907, at Sir Gaston Maspero's urging, Carnarvon collaborated with Howard Carter. Their association evolved into an abiding friendship, and the two worked in Egypt together for fifteen years, sharing the glory of the discovery of Tutankhamun's tomb. Carnarvon did not live to see the greatest treasures the tomb yielded up; he died of blood poisoning at the end of the first season. Carter dedicated his published report of the find to his friend:

> With the full sympathy of my collaborator, Mr. Mace, I dedicate this account of the discovery of the tomb of Tut Ankh Amun to the memory of my beloved friend and colleague, Lord Carnarvon, who died in the hour of his triumph. But for his untiring generosity and constant encouragement our labours could never have been crowned with success. His judgment in ancient art has rarely been equalled. His efforts, which have done so much to extend our knowledge of Egyptology, will ever be honoured in history, and by me his memory will always be cherished.

HARRY BURTON, 1879-1940

Burton, also English, joined the Museum's Egyptian Expedition
1914 after having worked with Theodore M. Davis in the Valley of th
Kings and at Medinet Habu in Thebes. His experience with archaec
ogical fieldwork and with photographing in European picture galle
ies served him well. The thousands of record photographs he took
the Egyptian necropolis are fascinating documents—straightforwar
detailed, yet compelling in the manner of the best photo-reportag
He was necessarily an improviser and mastered the primitive workir
conditions of the field: where electricity was not available he devise
a method of transmitting sunlight below ground by mirrors; in th
Valley of the Kings he created a darkroom by hanging blackout cu
tains in an empty tomb. The 1800 photographs he made during s
years of work at the tomb of Tutankhamun form an exciting narrati
of the discovery and are a remarkable achievement in science and a
Burton lived with his wife in Florence during the off-seasons and r
mained in charge of the Museum's affairs in Egypt until his death.

ARTHUR CRUTTENDON MACE, 1874-1928

Mace, an Englishman, joined the Egyptian Expedition at the beginning, in 1906, and became associate curator. He was widely experienced, having done fieldwork with Sir Flinders Petrie, George A. Reisner, and Lythgoe before taking on his assignment at the tomb of Tutankhamun: the on-site restoration of hundreds of treasures immediately as they were brought above ground. Mace was universally admired by his colleagues for the extreme care he took with his work. Lythgoe wrote to Carter regarding him: "I know of no one, without exception, to compare with him in the patient and painstaking skill necessary for the preservation of evidence and fragile material such as you have apparently in your present 'find.' His latest piece of work for us . . . was simply beyond all praise." Mace collaborated with Carter to write the official account of the discovery and worked with Carter in the Valley until his health failed in the summer of 1924.

ALBERT MORTON LYTHGOE, 1868-1934

The quintessential classics scholar, Lythgoe began his studies at the Classical High School of Providence, Rhode Island, and went on to Harvard and the American School of Classical Antiquities in Athens. He then taught at Harvard and was curator of Egyptian art at the Museum of Fine Arts, Boston. Lythgoe's early fieldwork (1899-1904) included several seasons with George A. Reisner on the Hearst Expedition of the University of California at Naga ed Deir. In 1906 he came to the Metropolitan Museum as the first curator of Egyptian art and founded the Egyptian Expedition. Upon his death, his great gift of organization and his enthusiasm were described by his student, friend, and colleague, H. E. Winlock:

> He was by nature a thorough and conscientious scientist and the expedition which he organized for the Metropolitan Museum was inspired by his zeal for the most accurate type of work possible. At the same time, he had a broader point of view on the function of an archaeological expedition than was usual a quarter of a century ago. He planned a program for the Metropolitan Museum which was to include excavations on sites of every period in the history of ancient Egypt, and also planned to conduct in conjunction with these excavations a survey of the monuments of Egypt to illustrate and supplement the excavated material.

Lythgoe was visiting in London when he received Carter's cabled request for help at the tomb of Tutankhamun. He eagerly lent the services of Burton, Mace, Hauser, and Hall, and he himself acted as liaison between Carter and the Egyptian officials during the first years of the work.

HERBERT EUSTIS WINLOCK, 1884-1950

Winlock was Lythgoe's student at Harvard and joined his mentor at the Metropolitan when the Egyptian Expedition was founded in 1906. The son of the assistant secretary of the Smithsonian Institution, Winlock was fascinated with Egyptian things from childhood and moved naturally into a career in archaeology. A man of great courtesy and a certain charming irreverence, he published widely and was widely read. His writings are marked by his wit and his ability to " 'retroject himself,' " as a colleague wrote in eulogy, "into a past civilization and make some of it come alive again for his contemporaries." In 1932 Winlock was named director of the Metropolitan. Though he clearly missed active fieldwork, his term as director was a distinguished one during which he received many honorary degrees and maintained a refreshing disdain for the pomp usually attending his office. He retired in 1939 to prepare his field notes for further publication. At the time of the discovery of Tutankhamun's tomb Winlock was director of the Museum's excavations at Sheik Abd el Qurna in western Thebes.

EDWARD ROBINSON, 1858-1931

Director of the Metropolitan at the time of the discovery, Robinson was a thoroughgoing classicist. His career in ancient art and archaeology began at Harvard, where he became a lecturer in classical antiquities after graduation. He became curator of classical antiquities and later director at the Museum of Fine Arts, Boston, before assuming the same roles at the Metropolitan. Under his directorship, which began in 1910, the Museum shed its image as a distinguished cast gallery and adopted the encyclopedic style of collecting that marks it today; five new departments emerged during Robinson's tenure—and the Egyptian Expedition flourished.

WALTER HAUSER, 1893-1959

Hauser was a true scholar with many talents and interests. He studied architecture at the Massachusetts Institute of Technology where he later taught both mathematics and drawing. After visiting Egypt he joined the Egyptian Expedition in 1919 and, with Lindsley Hall's assistance, was responsible for drafting the plans of the tomb of Tutankhamun. In his long career at the Museum Hauser served as surveyor and chief field assistant to Winlock in Egypt from 1921 to 1930 and worked on the joint excavations of the Museum and the German State Museums in Iraq at the Sasanian site of Ctesiphon. In 1932 he was adviser to the Persian Expedition of the Museum and was appointed curator of the Museum Library in 1946. A gifted editor, he spent his last four years on the staff as research curator of Near Eastern archaeology; in that capacity he published material gathered in the field in earlier years.

LINDSLEY FOOTE HALL

Hall came to work for the Egyptian Expedition in 1913 directly from the Massachusetts Institute of Technology where he had trained as an architectural draftsman. His meticulous drawings illustrated many publications of the Egyptian and Greek and Roman Art Departments. At the tomb of Tutankhamun his task was to help produce scale drawings indicating every item in the tangle of treasure—a staggering assignment which he fulfilled with characteristic care and accuracy.

Harry Burton:
The Archaeologist
as Photographer

*Burton wrote this piece for
the London* Times. *It was
carried by* The New York Times
on 15 February 1923

In view of the great interest that has been aroused by the discovery of the tomb of Tutankhamun by Lord Carnarvon and Mr. Howard Carter, a few notes on the photographic work in connection with the clearing may be of interest. Few people realize the importance of photography in archaeological research, but if it were not for the camera much evidence would be entirely lost, and certain details would never be noticed if photographs were not taken. Before excavations are commenced several general views of the site are taken, and it is from these that very useful information is obtained as to ground plans, which are frequently invisible to the naked eye yet are very distinct in a photograph.

FOREGROUND:
The entrance to the tomb

View along the road to the Valley
of the Kings

The work above ground is comparatively simple, as it is chiefly a question of choosing the right moment, i.e. when the light will give the best results of the site or objects to be photographed. Not so, however, in the work of photographing the interior of tombs where the light is, more often than not, practically nil, and the question is how to get it into the tomb to enable one to make an exposure. Until comparatively recently such photographs were taken with flashlight, but these were rarely satisfactory and, moreover, after one photograph had been taken it was necessary to wait a considerable time for the smoke to disperse before another could be taken. Only those who have taken flashlight photographs in an underground chamber can realize how long it takes for the smoke to clear away. It is therefore sheer waste of time to use flashlight if other means are available. I have had considerable experience in photographing the paintings and reliefs in the tombs of Thebes, and I have invariably succeeded, with a little management, in throwing sunlight into underground chambers—sometimes over 100 ft. below the surface—that have never before seen the light of day. This is done with the aid of large mirrors. One mirror is placed outside the tomb entrance in the sunshine, and the shaft of sunlight sent from this into the chamber is caught by a silver-papered reflector and thence thrown on to the part of the wall that is to be photographed, being kept constantly in motion to ensure equal lighting. Sometimes it is necessary to use two, or even three, mirrors in addition to the reflector, which adds to the work considerably, since the oftener the light is reflected the more it decreases in power and the longer it takes to make an exposure. The mirror outside is manipulated by one of the native camera boys who, in a long exposure of this kind, is liable to relax his attention and, unless constantly reminded, to let the sunshaft slip off the reflector.

When an intact tomb is found—unfortunately a very rare occurrence —one usually finds the entrance bricked up, and, in some cases, the entire surface of the plaster covered with seals. In such a case the first thing to be done is to photograph this sealed entrance, and nothing further must be done until the picture is developed and pronounced satisfactory. Duplicate negatives are invariably taken, as once the seals

Seal of the royal necropolis on the door of the burial chamber

and bricks are removed the photograph is the only evidence that remains. The entrance is then cleared, other general views are taken of the interior, and nothing is touched until satisfactory results have been obtained, as it is most important to have photographic records of how the objects were placed. These general views taken, the work of clearing begins and, as it progresses, detail photographs are taken of any new piece of evidence that turns up, or of any object or group of

The sealed door intact and (below) in the process of being dismantled

objects which the general views have failed to disclose. It may even, in some cases, be necessary to take a series of a dozen or more views of a single object in order to illustrate the various stages in its clearing or unwrapping. It sometimes happens that the photographs taken in the tomb are the only ones that it is possible to get, as frequently the objects collapse when touched. I remember when we were clearing a series of Seventeenth Dynasty tombs, which had been infested with white ants, the preliminary photographs were literally the only record of most of the wooden objects found. The coffins appeared to be in perfect condition, but when touched they collapsed into dust. There

CAMERA RECORDS DETAILS OF TOMB

Ivory and ebony casket no. 267 in situ in the treasury

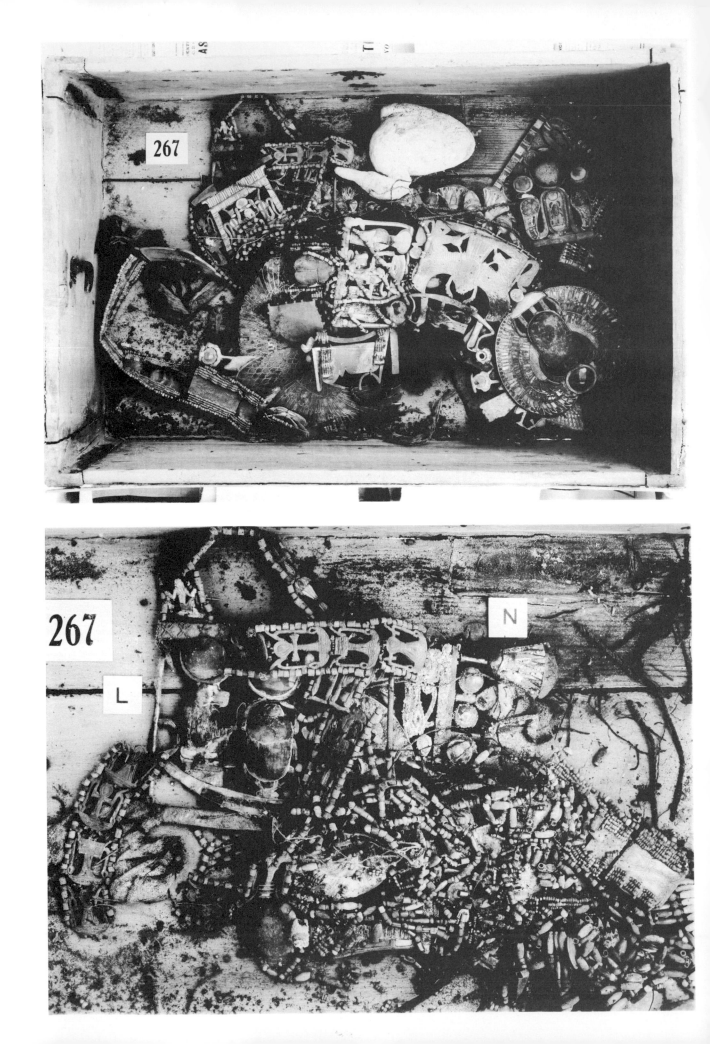

was one very attractive small wooden statuette of a girl in one of these tombs, which appeared to be quite sound. It was standing quite alone, and after the general view of the chamber had been taken the camera was turned on to it. I intended to expose a plate for two minutes, but after it had been exposed for 1¾ minutes the figure suddenly collapsed and nothing remained but a small heap of dust. I immediately switched off the beam of light, put a cap on the camera, and went off to develop the plate. Fortunately the negative turned out to be quite good, and although the statuette no longer existed we had a complete record of it. This is only one of many similar cases.

When Lord Carnarvon and Mr. Carter told me they were going to ask the Metropolitan Museum for the loan of my services to assist in the recording of the tomb of Tutankhamun the first idea that came to me was the question of lighting, and I was greatly relieved to learn that electric light was to be used and that we should be able to work independently of the sun. The Tombs of the Kings are lighted by electricity, so that it was only a question of extra wire and more powerful lamps. As a general rule one can rely on having bright sunshine at Luxor even in winter, but occasionally there are cloudy days which usually occur when least wanted.

Interior of casket no. 267 as opened and (below) after removal of top layer of jewelry

# The Find

The Valley and the Site

There is something about the atmosphere of Egypt— most people
experience it I think—that attunes one's mind to solitude.

The Valley of the Tombs of the Kings—the very name is full of romance, and of all Egypt's wonders there is none, I suppose, that makes a more instant appeal to the imagination. Here, in this lonely valley-head, remote from every sound of life, with the "Horn," the highest peak in the Theban hills, standing sentinel like a natural pyramid above them, lay thirty or more kings, among them the greatest Egypt ever knew.

At the beginning of the Eighteenth Dynasty there was hardly a king's tomb in the whole of Egypt that had not been rifled—a somewhat grisly thought to the monarch who was choosing the site for his own last resting place. Thutmose I evidently found it so, and devoted a good deal of thought to the problem, and as a result we get the lonely little tomb at the head of The Valley. Secrecy was to be the solution to the problem.

A preliminary step in this direction had been taken by his predecessor, Amenhotpe I, who made his tomb some distance away from his

funerary temple, on the summit of the Diraa Abu-n-Naga foot-hills,
hidden beneath a stone, but this was carrying it a good deal further.
Now there was to be no monument over the tomb itself, and the
funerary temple in which the offerings were made was to be situated
a mile or so away, on the other side of the hill. It was certainly not a
convenient arrangement, but it was necessary if the secrecy of the
tomb was to be kept, and secrecy King Thutmose had decided on, as
the one chance of escaping the fate of his predecessors.

How long the secret of this particular tomb held we do not know. Probably not long, for what secret was ever kept in Egypt? At the time of its discovery in 1899 little remained in it but the massive stone sarcophagus, and the king himself was moved, as we know, first of all to the tomb of his daughter Hatshepsut, and subsequently, with the other royal mummies to Deir el Bahri. In any case, whether the hiding of the tomb was temporarily successful or not, a new fashion had been set, and the remaining kings of this Dynasty, together with those of the Nineteenth and Twentieth, were all buried in The Valley.

The idea of secrecy did not long prevail. From the nature of things it could not, and the later kings seem to have accepted the fact, and gone back to the old plan of making their tombs conspicuous. Now that it had become the established custom to place all the royal tombs within a very restricted area they may have thought that tomb-robbery was securely provided against, seeing that it was very much to the reigning king's interest to see that the royal burial site was protected. If they did, they mightily deceived themselves. We know from internal evidence that Tutankhamun's tomb was entered by robbers [after] his death.

For a few generations, under the powerful kings of the Eighteenth and Nineteenth Dynasties, The Valley tombs must have been reasonably secure. Plundering on a big scale would be impossible without the connivance of the officials concerned. In the Twentieth Dynasty it was quite another story. There were weaklings on the throne, a fact of which the official classes, as ever, were quick to take advantage. Cemetery guardians became lax and venial, and a regular orgy of grave-robbing seems to have set in.

Throughout all the troublous times in the Twentieth and Twenty-first Dynasties there is no mention of Tutankhamun and his tomb. He had not escaped altogether—his tomb, as we have already noted, having been entered within years of his death—but he was lucky enough to escape the ruthless plundering of the later period. For some reason his tomb had been overlooked. It was situated in a very low-lying part of The Valley, and a heavy rain storm might well have washed away all trace of its entrance. Or again, it may owe its safety to the fact that a number of huts, for the use of workmen who were employed in excavating the tomb of a later king, were built immediately above it.

Yet, plundered, deserted and desolate as were its tombs, the romance of [the Valley] was not yet wholly gone. It still remained the sacred Valley of the Kings, and crowds of the sentimental and the curious must still have gone to visit it.

November 1922

This was to be our final season in The Valley. Six full seasons we had excavated there, and season after season had drawn a blank; we had worked for months at a stretch and found nothing, and only an excavator knows how desperately depressing that can be; we had almost made up our minds that we were beaten, and were preparing to leave The Valley and try our luck elsewhere; and then—hardly had we set hoe to ground in our last despairing effort than we made a discovery that far exceeded our wildest dreams.

Our former excavations had stopped short at the north-east corner of the tomb of Ramesses VI, and from this point I started trenching southwards. . . . In this area there were a number of roughly constructed workmen's huts, used probably by the labourers in the tomb of Ramesses. By the evening of November 3rd we had laid bare a sufficient number of these huts for experimental purposes, so, after we

had planned and noted them, they were removed, and we were ready to clear away the three feet of soil that lay beneath them.

Hardly had I arrived on the work next morning (November 4th) than the unusual silence, due to the stoppage of the work, made me realize that something out of the ordinary had happened, and I was greeted by the announcement that a step cut in the rock had been discovered underneath the very first hut to be attacked.

Work continued feverishly throughout the whole of that day and the morning of the next, but it was not until the afternoon of November 5th that we succeeded in clearing away the masses of rubbish that overlay the cut, and were able to demarcate the upper edges of the stairway on all its four sides.

Work progressed more rapidly now; step succeeded step, and at the level of the twelfth, towards sunset, there was disclosed the upper part of a doorway, blocked, plastered, and sealed.

26

A sealed doorway—it was actually true, then! Our years of patient labour were to be rewarded after all. . . .

It was a thrilling moment for an excavator. Alone, save for my native workmen, I found myself, after years of comparatively unproductive labour, on the threshold of what might prove to be a magnificent discovery. Anything, literally anything, might lie beyond that passage, and it needed all my self-control to keep from breaking down the doorway, and investigating then and there.

. . . Thirty feet down from the outer door, we came upon a second sealed doorway, almost an exact replica of the first. . . . Slowly, desperately slowly it seemed to us as we watched, the remains of passage debris that encumbered the lower part of the doorway were removed, until at last we had the whole door clear before us. The decisive moment had arrived. With trembling hands I made a tiny breach in the upper left hand corner. Darkness and blank space, as far as an iron testing-rod could reach, showed that whatever lay beyond was empty, and not filled like the passage we had just cleared. Candle tests were applied as a precaution against possible foul gases, and then, widening the hole a little, I inserted the candle and peered in. . . . At first I could see nothing, the hot air escaping from the chamber causing the candle flame to flicker, but presently, as my eyes grew accustomed to the light, details of the room within emerged slowly from the mist, strange animals, statues, and gold—everywhere the glint of gold. For the moment—an eternity it must have seemed to the others standing by—I was struck dumb with amazement, and when Lord Carnarvon, unable to stand the suspense any longer, inquired anxiously, "Can you see anything?" it was all I could do to get out the words, "Yes, wonderful things."

The Antechamber

There was a certain amount of confusion, it was true,
but it was orderly confusion . . .

Turning right as we entered, we noticed, first, a large cylindrical jar of alabaster; next, two funerary bouquets of leaves, one leaning against the wall, the other fallen; and in front of them, standing out into the chamber, a painted wooden casket. This last will probably rank as one of the greatest artistic treasures of the tomb, and on our first visit we found it hard to tear ourselves away from it. Its outer surface was completely covered with gesso; upon this prepared surface there were a series of brilliantly coloured and exquisitely painted designs—hunting scenes upon the curved panels of the lid, battle scenes upon the sides, and upon the ends representations of the king in lion form, trampling his enemies under his feet. The illustrations give but a faint idea of the delicacy of the painting, which far surpasses anything ot the kind that Egypt has yet produced.

The quality of the material so far brought to light simply defies de-
scription. The character and workmanship of each individual object,
whatever the material, is so exquisitely fine that it places Egyptian art
on a level we had never previously comprehended. After hours spent
in examining it, piece by piece, I could only drive home last evening
in silence—utterly incapable of putting my thoughts and impressions
into words.

Letter, Lythgoe to Robinson, 1 February 1923

The motifs are Egyptian and the treatment Egyptian, and yet they leave an impression on your mind of something strangely non-Egyptian, and you cannot for the life of you explain exactly where the difference lies. They remind you of other things too—the finest Persian miniatures, for instance....

Turning now to the long (west) wall of the chamber, we found the whole of the wall-space occupied by the three great animal-sided couches, curious pieces of furniture which we knew from illustrations in the tomb paintings, but of which we had never seen actual examples before. The first was lion-headed, the second cow-headed, and the third had the head of a composite animal, half hippopotamus and half crocodile.

TOMB TREASURES REVISE OUR IDEAS OF ANCIENT EGYPT

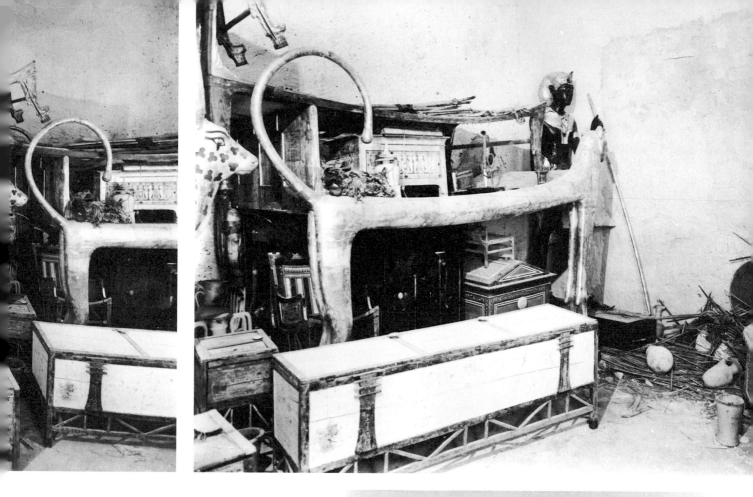

The couch is a most gorgeous and barbaric piece of royal furniture. The word couch to us conveys something low and informal, but this one stands four and a half or five feet....

[These] are fearsome dog heads, prototypes of the Cerberus-like Great Danes with a lion strain. Like all else they are gilt, with open mouths, from which long curling tongues of ivory-colored pink protrude and ivory teeth [these white] set wide apart. The carving of the heads is very bold and the gilding is in excellent condition, though some other parts of the couch are less good....

The New York Times,
1 February 1923

Below [the hippopotamus/crocodile-headed] couch stood another o
the great artistic treasures of the tomb—a throne, overlaid with gol
from top to bottom, and richly adorned with glass, faience and ston
inlay. Its legs, fashioned in feline form, were surmounted by lion:
heads, fascinating in their strength and simplicity. Magnificer
crowned and winged serpents formed the arms, and between the bar
which supported the back there were six protective cobras, carved i
wood, gilt and inlaid. . . . I have no hesitation in claiming for it that
is the most beautiful thing that has yet been found in Egypt.

The seat is intricately inlaid, but its greatest beauty is the back, which is inlaid with pictures of the King and Queen in their royal robes of truly thrilling beauty. The flesh portions of the figures seem to be cornelian, while the ornaments, dresses, head-dresses, embroideries and so forth are all rendered in exquisitely fine inlaying of semi-precious stones.

The New York Times,
23 January 1923

Clearing the objects from the antechamber was like playing a gigantic game of spillikins. So crowded were they that it was a matter of extreme difficulty to move one without running serious risk of damaging others, and in some cases they were so inextricably tangled that an elaborate system of props and supports had to be devised to hold one object or group of objects in place while others were being removed. At such times life was a nightmare. One was afraid to move lest one should kick against a prop and bring the whole thing crashing down.

. . . Working from north to south, and thus putting off the evil day when we would have to tackle the complicated tangle of chariots, we gradually disencumbered the great animal couches of the objects which surrounded them. Each object as it was removed was placed upon a padded wooden stretcher and securely fastened to it with bandages. Enormous numbers of these stretchers were required, for, to avoid double handling, they were in almost every case left permanently with the object, and not re-used. From time to time, when a sufficient number of stretchers had been filled—about once a day, on an average—a convoy was made up and dispatched under guard to the laboratory.

PHARAOH'S SANDALS MAY SET NEW STYLE

Some of the King's sandals are perfectly wonderful, though difficult to describe. The leather has entirely perished and turned into a black glue-like substance. The glue is just keeping the decorations together.... When these sandals have been restored they will be among the most wonderful articles in all this mass of extraordinary works of art, and I fully expect that in a few years' time we shall see our smartest ladies wearing footgear more or less resembling and absolutely inspired by these wonderful things.

An unidentified observer in
The New York Times,
31 January 1923

The Burial Chamber

Are we . . . when that sealed doorway is opened, to behold a sight beyond anything that Egypt has ever yielded up to archaeological research?

Letter, Lythgoe to Robinson, 1 February 1923

READY FOR OPENING OF INNER CHAMBER OF PHARAOH'S TOMB

Carter first drove his cold-chisel in at the point where he thought he could detect the presence of a wooden beam serving as lintel of the door, and he found it successfully. Then he began gradually to cut down. It must have been some ten minutes before he had an opening perhaps a foot wide and eight or ten inches high, through which he could look with the aid of an electric torch. We all stood expectant— one could have heard a pin drop—and he finally said, "I see, quite close, what appears to be the side of a great shrine or catafalque of blue faience and gold." Then each of us in turn looked through and saw it, so near that one could almost touch it. And what a sight it was, for then we knew that for the first time among all the discoveries which had ever been made in Egypt, we had preserved to us the sepulchre and funerary paraphernalia of an Egyptian King—intact so far as its arrangements were concerned, even if it proved to have been violated to some extent by ancient plunderers.

And yet, I myself felt nothing of nervous excitement—it was all too stupendously awe-inspiring for that. For the first time in all my experience of looking into and finally entering ancient burial chambers, I felt the presence of the dead.

Letter, Lythgoe to Robinson, 22 February 1923

Carter dropped into the chamber and disappeared from sight along the passage to the right, starting towards what was obviously the front end of the catafalque, to judge from the up-slope of its roof as we saw it from side-view through the doorway.

Letter, Lythgoe to Robinson, 22 February 1923

Resting upon the ground, between the shrine and the north wall, were magic oars to ferry the king's barque across the waters of the Nether World. . . .

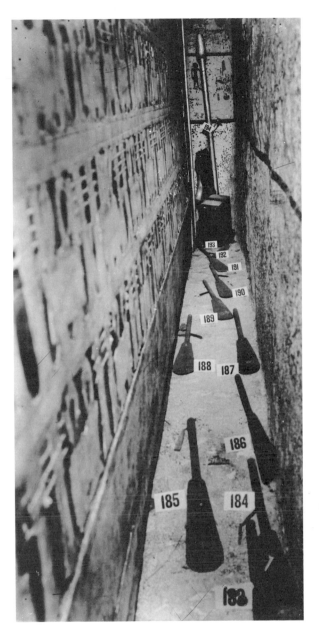

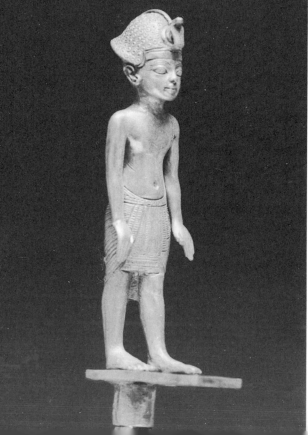

We all (ladies and everybody) saw Carter unwrap the large bundles of staves found between the 1st and 2nd catafalques the beginning of the season. Harkness and I looked over some of them again yesterday with Carter—they are finer in every respect than those found in the antechamber last season. Two of them, one of gold and one of silver, some three feet in length, are surmounted by identical (practically) statuettes of the king—represented clearly as a chubby boy.

Letter, Lythgoe to Robinson, 1 February 1924

Mr. Carter was perched on the elaborate scaffolding which has been erected about the canopy, busily engaged with a pencil, drawing block and yard measure in planning the next steps in the work of taking down the shrines. He drew the attention of the correspondents to the many evidences of hasty or careless work on the part of the joiners or undertakers who thirty-two centuries ago by the light of smoky lamps assembled the four shrines about the great crystalline sarcophagus containing the Pharaoh's mummy.

The New York Times,
14 January 1924

After our scaffolding and hoisting tackle had been introduced it occupied practically all the available space, leaving little for ourselves in which to work. When some of the parts were freed, there was insufficient room to remove them from the chamber. We bumped our heads, nipped our fingers, we had to squeeze in and out like weasels, and work in all kinds of embarrassing positions. I think I remember that one of the eminent chemists assisting us in the preservation work, when taking records of various phenomena in the tomb, found that he had also recorded a certain percentage of profanity! Nevertheless, I am glad to say that in the conflict we did more harm to ourselves than to the shrines.

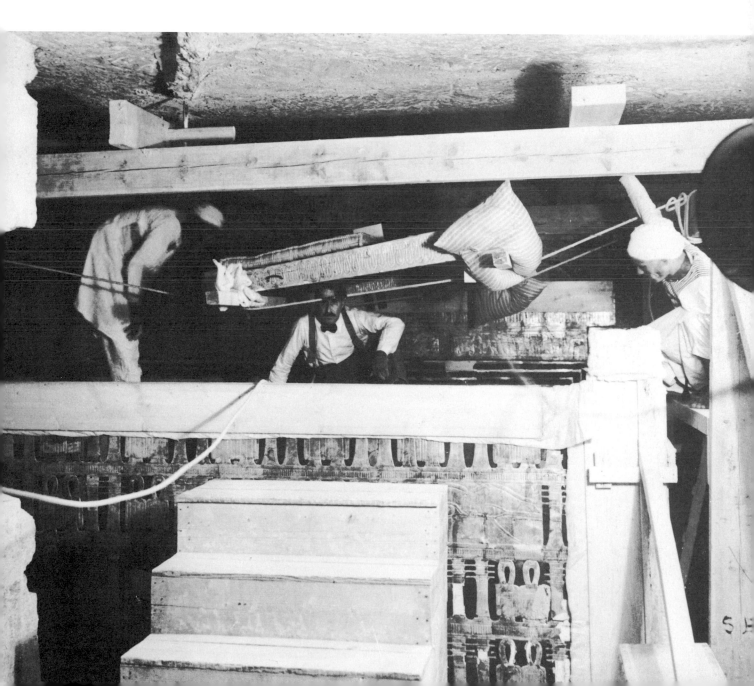

The pall made us realize that we were in the presence of a dead kin
of past ages. The unbroken seal upon the closed doors of the secon
shrine gave us the data we were seeking. Had the tomb-robbers, wh
had entered the antechamber, its annex, the burial chamber and i
storeroom by any chance reached the king? The shrine was intact, i
doors bore their original seal uninjured, indicating that the robbe
had not reached him. Henceforth, we knew that, within the shrin
we should be treading where no one had entered, and that we shou
be dealing with material untouched and unharmed since the boy kin
was laid to rest nearly three thousand three hundred years ago.

When we drew back those ebony bolts of the great shrine, the doo
swung back as if only closed yesterday, and revealed within y
another shrine, in type like the first save for the blue inlay. It ha
similar bolted doors, but upon them was a seal intact, bearing th
name of Tutankhamun and a recumbent jackal over Egypt's nine foe

*Words can never describe my sensations as I stood there, literal.
bewildered by it all. Those great doors of the catafalque, standin
ajar, and, close inside, the sealed doors of the inner one! Inside c
that, shall we eventually come on another one, and another an
another, and then the sarcophagus and its sets of gilded coffins? Yo
can see the possibilities still in store for us—*

Letter, Lythgoe to Robinson, 22 February 192

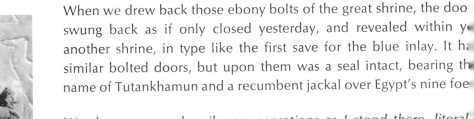

The shrine, dazzling from the brilliance of its gold, was decorated with scenes wrought, in beautiful incised-relief, from the book "Of that which is in the Underworld"—that guide to the Hereafter, which points out to the deceased the road he should take, and explains to him the various malefic powers he must meet during his subterranean journey. According to this book, two routes led him to the land of the blessed, one by water, the other by land, and it further shows that there were by-ways leading to seething rivers of fire by which he must not travel.

One may well imagine the thrill of awe felt by Mr. Howard Carter and his associates, when, on January 3, they saw for the first time the sarcophagus of Tutankhamun standing where it was placed 3200 years ago. "There have been two such moments," said the official record: "one when the tomb was originally opened . . . and the second when the sealed door was broken through. . . . One more such moment awaits us, when we shall be enabled to raise the sarcophagus lid and see the King in all the majesty of death within."

The Illustrated London News,
26 January 1924

The tackle for raising the lid was in position. I gave the word. Amid intense silence the huge slab, broken in two, weighing over a ton and a quarter, rose from its bed. The light shone into the sarcophagus. A sight met our eyes that at first puzzled us. It was a little disappointing. The contents were completely covered by fine linen shrouds. The lid being suspended in mid-air, we rolled back those covering shrouds, one by one, and as the last was removed a gasp of wonderment escaped our lips, so gorgeous was the sight that met our eyes: a golden effigy of the young boy king, of most magnificent workmanship, filled the whole of the interior of the sarcophagus.

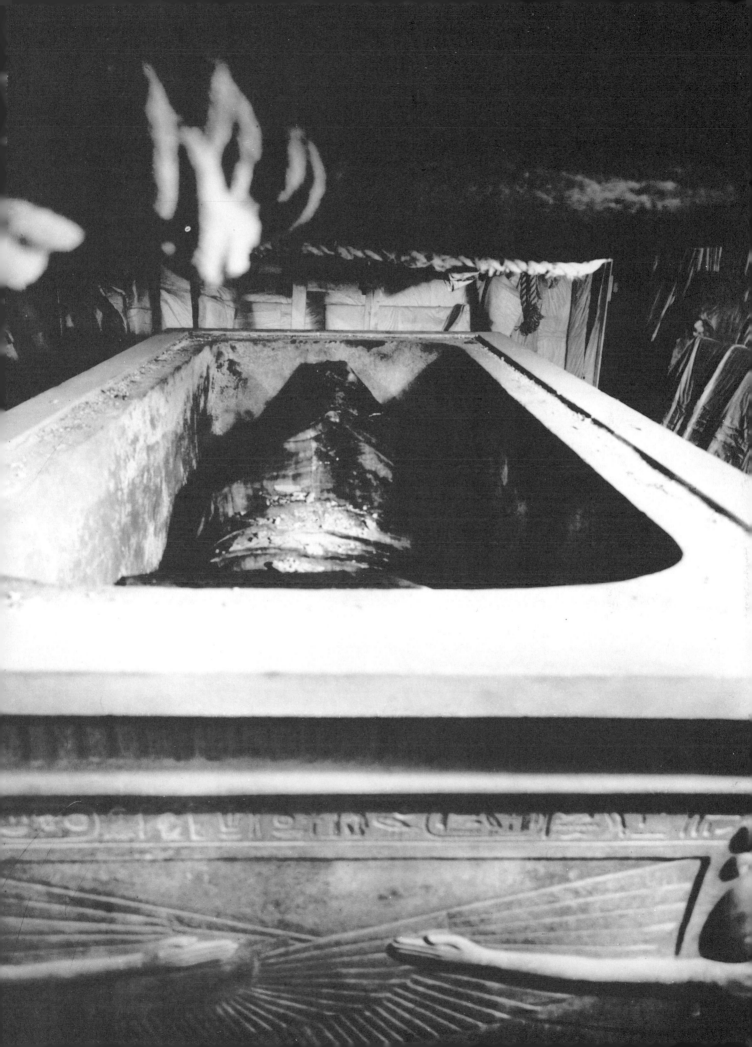

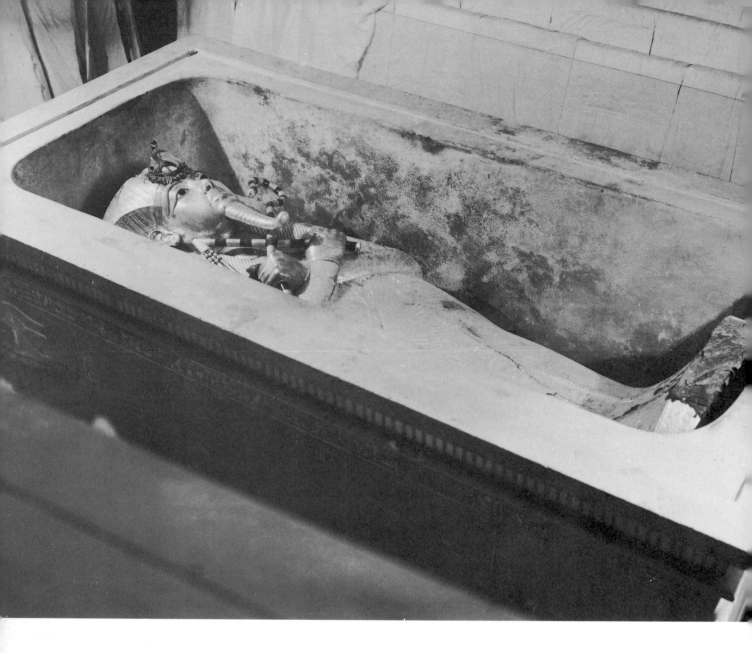

The gilt inner coffin of Pharaoh Tutankhamun, built to the shape of the
young King and bearing an exquisite representation of him, has been
uncovered by Howard Carter and
his associates.

This was revealed in an official
announcement today telling of the
progress at the tomb since work began on Oct. 12. When the outer
sarcophagus was opened, the com-
muniqué says, a second sarcophagus
was disclosed, bearing on top a representation of the god Osiris and entirely covered from head to foot with
painted designs and glass of many
colors on a surface of gold with a
marble background. On the body
of this second sarcophagus were
painted figures of Nekhbet, the goddess of Upper Egypt, and Wadjet,
the goddess of night.

FACE OF PHARAOH
FINALLY EXPOSED

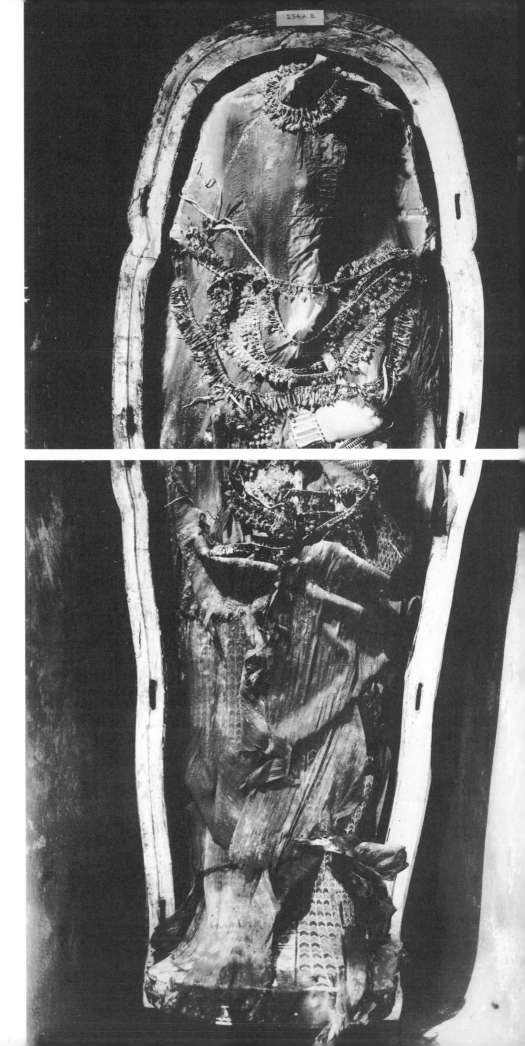

After the second sarcophagus was scientifically examined and lifted out the cover was removed and it revealed the gilt-covered human-shaped inner coffin, but the details of its design were covered by a linen shroud which adhered closely. About it was an exquisite necklace, and flowers were tied to the head bandage and were reposing on the breast. The head of the coffin was uncovered and the likeness of the young Pharaoh was seen.

After photographing the contents of the second sarcophagus, the necklace and linen shroud were removed, revealing the beautiful coffin covered with gold ornamentations of marvelous workmanship, but, unfortunately, most of the detail is covered with a black glutinous layer from the libations at the original funeral ceremonies.

The most important part of the work now is the removal of this glutinous layer and the lifting of the human-shaped coffin from the second sarcophagus, to which it is closely sticking, owing to the libational deposit.

The New York Times,
6 November 1925

Familiarity can never entirely dissipate the feeling of mystery—the sense of vanished but haunting forces that cling to the tomb. The conviction of the unity of past and present is constantly impressed upon the archaeological adventurer, even when absorbed in the mechanical details of his work.

In spite of the great weight of the coffins—far heavier than at first seemed possible—they were successfully raised to just above the level of the top of the sarcophagus, when wooden planks were passed under them. In the confined space, and with the restricted head-room available, the task proved one of no little difficulty. It was much increased by the necessity of avoiding damage to the fragile gesso-gilt surfaces of the outermost coffin.

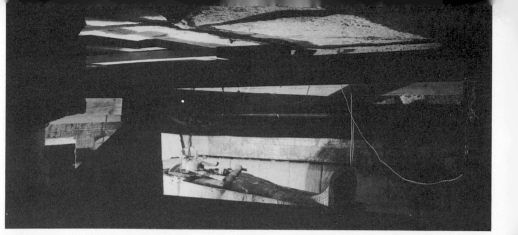

Mr. Burton at once made his photographic records. I then removed the floral collarette and linen coverings. An astounding fact was disclosed. This third coffin, 6 feet 1¾ of an inch in length, was made of solid gold! The mystery of the enormous weight, which hitherto had puzzled us, was now clear. It explained also why the weight had diminished so slightly after the first coffin, and the lid of the second coffin, had been removed. Its weight was still as much as eight strong men could lift.

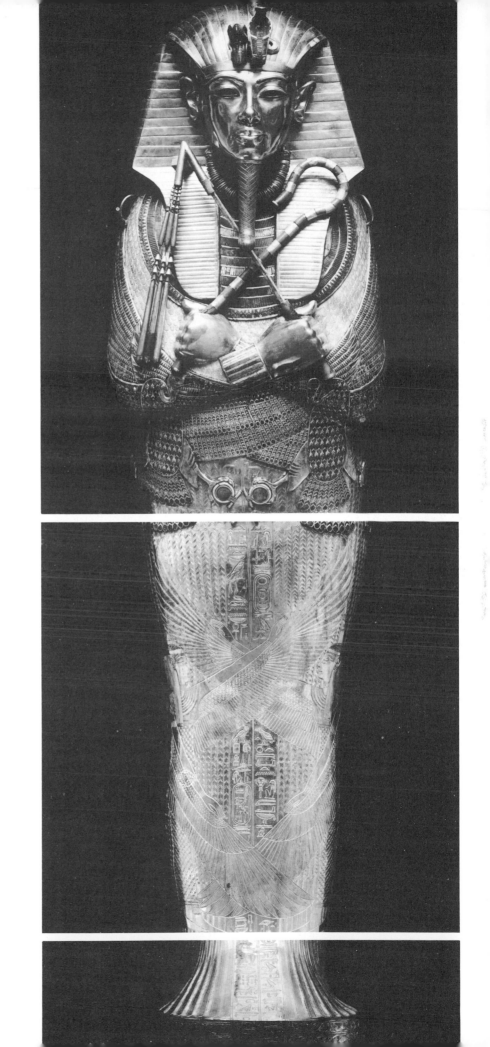

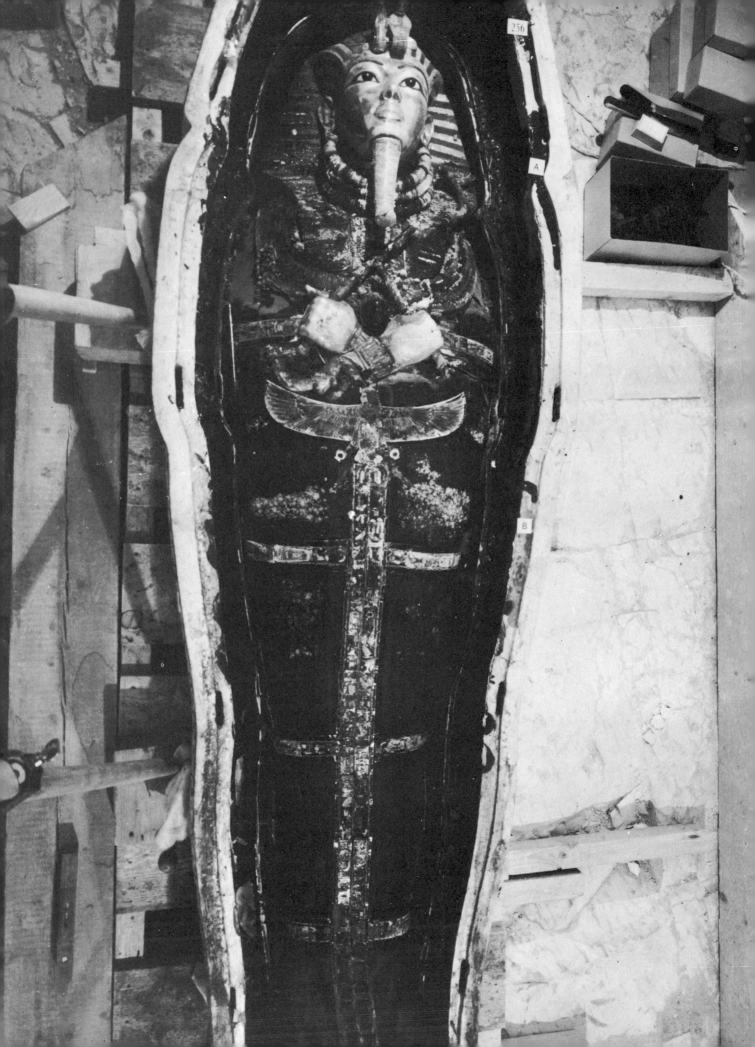

. . . The lid was raised by its golden handles and the mummy of the king disclosed. At such moments the emotions evade verbal expression, complex and stirring as they are. Three thousand years and more had elapsed since men's eyes had gazed into the golden coffin. Time, measured by the brevity of human life, seemed to lose its common perspectives before a spectacle so vividly recalling the solemn religious rites of a vanished civilization. But it is useless to dwell on such sentiments, based as they are on feelings of awe and human pity. The emotional side is no part of archaeological research. Here at last lay all that was left of the youthful Pharaoh, hitherto little more to us than the shadow of a name.

Before us, occupying the whole of the interior of the golden coffin, was an impressive, neat and carefully made mummy, over which had been poured anointing unguents as in the case of the outside of its coffin—again in great quantity—consolidated and blackened by age.

The beaten gold mask, a beautiful and unique specimen of ancient portraiture, bears a sad but calm expression suggestive of youth overtaken prematurely by death.

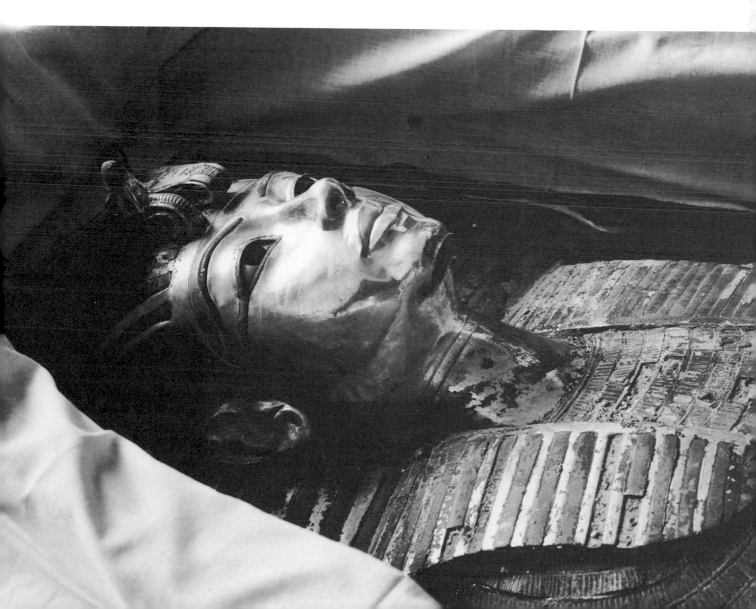

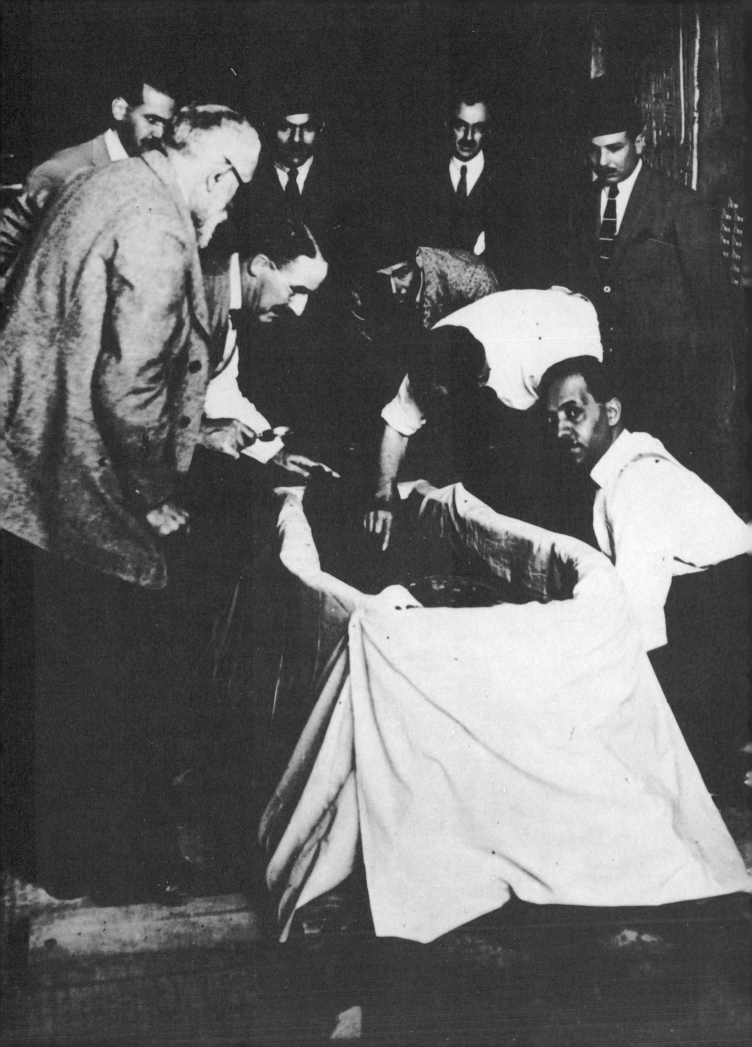

Howard Carter, in the presence of Prof. Lacau, French director of antiquities, and the Egyptian Government doctors, continued today his examination of the mummy of King Tutankhamun.

The World.
12 November 1925

Is there any chance of your wanting an anatomist on your new find? You know I am specially interested, as I have measured up and reported on Akhenaton whom [M. Georges] Daressy says is Tutankhamun. This discovery puts the lid on that theory I imagine. . . .

Letter to Carter from Dr. Douglas Derry, Professor of Anatomy at Egyptian University, who examined the royal mummy

The removal of the final wrappings that protected the face of the king needed the utmost care, as owing to the carbonized state of the head there was always the risk of injury to the very fragile features. We realized the peculiar importance and responsibility attached to our task. At the touch of a sable brush the last few fragments of decayed fabric fell away, revealing a serene and placid countenance, that of a young man.

The Treasury

Small and simple, as it is, the impressive memories of the past haunt
it none the less . . . .

Placed in the doorway, practically preventing ingress to the recess, was a black and gold figure of the jackal Anubis, swathed in linen, couchant, upon a gilt pylonic shrine fixed upon carrying poles. Within the threshold, in front of Anubis, was a small reed torch upon a clay brick. And, behind Anubis, a strange head of a cow—emblems these of the Netherworld where the sun sinks and the dead rest.

Letter, Carter to Mrs. Edward Robinson, 10 February 1927

The reed torch—the Sacred Flame—was not dropped upon the floor haphazardly within the threshold. It was placed there to repel the enemy of the deceased, in whatever form he may come. The incantation scratched upon its brick says: "It is I who hinder the sand from choking the secret chamber. I cause the path to be mistaken. I am for the protection of the deceased."

Letter, Carter to Mrs. Robinson, 10 February 1927

Facing the doorway, on the farther side, stood the most beautiful monument that I have ever seen—so lovely that it made one gasp with wonder and admiration. The central portion of it consisted of a large shrine-shaped chest, completely overlaid with gold, and surmounted by a cornice of sacred cobras. Surrounding this, freestanding, were statues of the four tutelary goddesses of the dead—gracious figures with outstretched protective arms, so natural and lifelife in their pose, so pitiful and compassionate the expression upon their faces, that one felt it almost sacrilege to look at them.

The contents of the little store-chamber in front of the catafalque would alone count as the most momentous discovery ever previously made. For example, against the rear wall of this chamber stands a great golden shrine some 7 feet high and 3 wide x 4 deep—with closed double doors—which must contain the canopic box and jars, for outside, on each side, upon the projecting ledge on the bottom, stand the four protective divinities, Isis, Nephthys, Neith and Selket, each golden figure quite 3 feet high, standing with outstretched arms in protective attitude, their heads turned sidewise and upwards, their exquisite faces and figures more beautiful than one dreamed human hands could produce.

Letter, Lythgoe to Robinson, 22 February 1923

The alabaster Canopic chest certainly proves to be one of the most beautiful objects among the funerary equipment of the king. Shrine-like in form, it has the usual entablature common to the design, its sides have a slight "batter" and on the corners the four guardian goddesses are carved in high-relief—Isis on the south-west corner, Nephthys on the north-west corner, Neith on the south-east corner, and Selket on the north-east corner. On each side are their respective formulae in bold hieroglyphics, incised and filled in with dark blue pigment. The massive lid, which forms the entablature, was carefully secured to the chest by means of cord bound to gold staples and sealed with the design: a recumbent figure of the Anubis jackal-like beast over the nine races of mankind in prisoner form, in fact, the device of the royal necropolis seal.

The interior of the chest was only carved out some five inches deep, but sufficiently to give the appearance of four rectangular compartments containing each a jar. Covering the tops of each of the imitation jars were separate human-headed lids, finely sculptured in alabaster in the likeness of the king. The two on the east side faced west, and the two on the west side faced east. The rebated flanges of the human-headed lids fitted into the openings of the counterfeit jars: that is to say they covered the mouths of the four cylindrical holes in the chest which took the place of real jars. In each hollow, wrapped in linen, was an exquisite miniature gold coffin, elaborately inlaid and resembling the second coffin of the king.

These miniature coffins which held the viscera are wonderful specimens of both goldsmith's and jeweller's art. They are replicas of the second coffin that enclosed the king, but far more elaborately inlaid in feather design, the burnished gold faces being the only part of the figures that has been left plain. Each bears down the front the formula pertaining to the goddess and her genius to which it belongs, and each has on the interior surfaces beautifully engraved texts pertaining to the rite.

Every box we open brings forth new and unexpected treasures, and I may say that we are almost overwhelmed with the material.

Letter, Carter to Mrs. Albert M. Lythgoe, 5 January 1923

Along the south wall, extending from east to west, stood a large quantity of black, sinister, shrine-like chests, all closed and sealed save one, the folding doors of which had fallen apart revealing statuettes of the king, swathed in linen, standing on the backs of black leopards. Since the discovery, imagination faltered at the thought of what those other chests might contain. The time has come when we are soon to know.

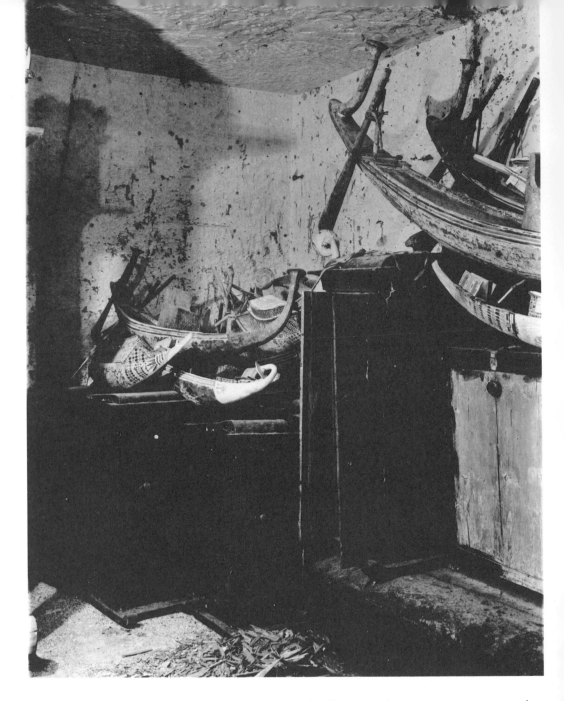

Stacked on top of those black chests, without any apparent order, save that their stems all pointed west, were a number of model craft, equipped with cabins, look-outs, thrones and kiosks, upon the poop, the amidship, and after-decks; and in front of the chests, resting upon a wooden model of a granary filled with grain, was another and more elaborate boat with rigging and furled sail.

Among the interesting discoveries in the third chamber was a flotilla of eighteen boats, presumably an ancient custom of providing the dead with transport to Heaven.

Another discovery was a number of beautifully carved human figures to serve as substitutes for the dead in the event that Osiris, divine king of the dead, imposed tasks of penitence upon the new arrivals, perhaps not befitting the dignity of an earthly king.

The New York Times.
5 February 1928

The Annex

The only present access to this apartment is a small hole close to the
ground, still half concealed by the
sole remaining royal couch. This
hole was made by robbers and is
large enough to admit the head and
shoulders of a man. The only view
of the interior of this apartment yet
obtained has been by a privileged
few who have been permitted to
crawl under the couch and put their
heads through the hole, holding an
electric bulb in their hands.

The New York Times
7 February 1923

Then, remember, that the 2nd antechamber is piled up quite five to six feet high over most of its area with masses of objects of every type and material you could imagine—

Letter, Lythgoe to Robinson, 1 February 192

The fourth chamber was discovered in 1922 but was sealed up until work in other portions of the tomb was finished. The chamber is devoid of mural inscriptions, engravings or paintings and the contents are jumbled in a hopeless fashion. . . .

The New York Times,
9 January 1928

Among the series of ornamental caskets, a much ill-treated but wonderful specimen was found at the northern end of the chamber. The lid was thrown in one corner, while the empty casket itself was heaved into another....

The central panel of the lid is certainly the unsigned work of a master.... It depicts the young king and queen in a pavilion bedecked with vines and festoons of flowers. The royal couple, wearing floral collarettes and dressed in semi-court attire, face one another; the king, leaning slightly on his staff, accepts from his consort bouquets of papyrus and lotus-blooms; while, in a frieze below, two court maidens gather flowers and the fruit of the mandrake for their charges. Above their Majesties are short inscriptions: *"The Beautiful God, Lord of the Two Lands, Neb-khepru-Ra, Tut-ankh-Amun, Ruler of the Southern Heliopolis [Thebes], resembling Ra." "The Great-Royal-Wife, Lady of the Two Lands, Ankh-es-en-Amun, May she live."*

Unfortunately, the ostrich-feathers of all [the] fans were so decayed that only in a few cases the shafts of the feathers remained, and they again were in such a bad condition that it was almost impossible to preserve them. However, there were sufficient remains to show us that the flabellate or palmate tops of the fan-stocks, into which the quills were fixed, once held 48 feathers (i.e. 24 on each side), and that the shafts of the feathers had been stripped of their "vanes" for a short distance above the quills, so that a portion of the bare shafts was visible, like radii, and, thus, must have resembled the radiating framework ("sticks") of the modern folding fan.

Stacked on top of the stone vessels and the pottery wine-jars were 116 baskets, or even more, if the baskets of similar make that were found discarded on the floor of the antechamber be included. They contained foodstuffs—mostly sundry fruits and seeds, including the mandrake, *nabakh,* grapes, dates, melon seeds, and *dôm*-nuts.

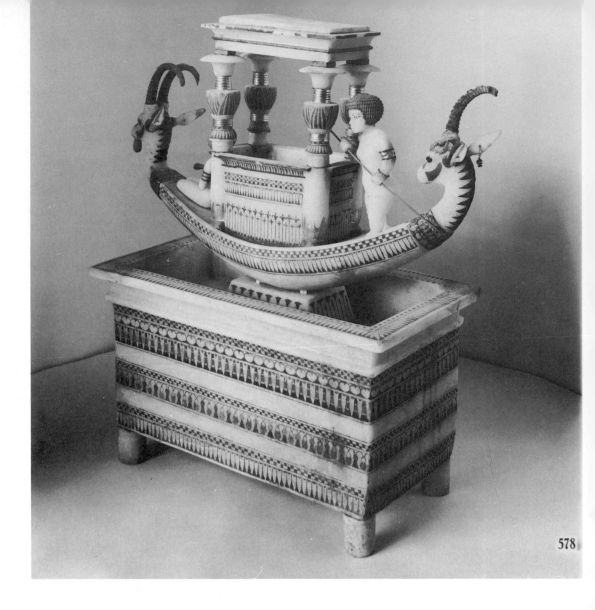

578

A most remarkable and fragile object wrought of alabaster (calcite) stood upon the floor almost unscathed. It takes the form of a boat floating in an ornamental tank. I have named it a "centre-piece" (for what else could it be?) carved of semi-translucent alabaster, engraved and painted with chaplets of fruit and flowers, as if to figure at a banquet or celebration of some kind. There is something extremely fanciful about it, as well as interesting, for is it not but another glimpse into the faded past breaking forth from the gloom of the tomb?

Facing forward, on the fore-deck, is a charming little figure of a nude girl, squatting and holding a lotus flower to her breast. At the helm, steering the boat, is a puny slave, which brings to mind the dwarfs at the helms of the Phoenician ships mentioned by Herodotus. . . . A mere glance at the photograph suffices to realize how beautifully, and how accurately, both of these female figures and the ibex heads have been rendered by the court stone-carver who wrought this fascinating ornament.

Epilogue

At all times and on all races, death has loomed as the most tremendous mystery and the last inevitable necessity that man's obscure destiny must face—and pathetic have been his efforts to throw light on the darkness shrouding his future. His life and art were once mainly concerned with this insoluble problem. Human reason has always attempted to calm human fears; man's mind, yearning and active, has instinctively endeavored to find in his beliefs solace for them—to call up some protection against the dangers that fill the dark gulf of the Unknown. But one touching glimmer of hope has always shone through the gloom. On the threshold of death he has always sought comfort in the love and affection which he hoped would knit him to the living—a natural yearning revealed in the ancient burial rituals.

My task has been not only to preserve, but to leave nothing unexplored that might add to the sum of our steadily growing knowledge of this deeply interesting and complicated funerary cult. I also trust that this rambling account of our investigations has not bored you. . . .

Letter, Carter to Mrs. Edward Robinson, 10 February 1927